coast-to-coast cycle route
between Morecambe and Bridlington
170 miles (274km)

Way of the **Roses**

Rupert Douglas

sustrans
JOIN THE MOVEMENT

We have taken all reasonable steps to ensure that the route described in this book is safe and achievable by people with a reasonable level of fitness. However, all outdoor activities involve a degree of risk and the publishers accept no responsibility for any injuries caused to readers while following the Way of the Roses.

The contents of this book are believed correct at the time of printing. Nevertheless, the publishers cannot be held responsible for any errors or omissions or for changes in the details given in this book or for the consequences of any reliance on the information provided by the same. This does not affect your statutory rights.

Published by Sustrans
2 Cathedral Square, College Green,
Bristol BS1 5DD
www.sustrans.org.uk

ISBN 978-1-90-138988-3

Text and photography copyright ©sustrans 2013

Maps contain Ordnance Survey data
© Crown copyright and database right [2013].

Sustrans is a Registered Charity in the UK: Number 326550 (England and Wales) SCO39263 (Scotland).

Designed by Cooper Douglas Partnership
Printed in England

Foreword

Whatever the historic rivalry between the two noble counties of Yorkshire and Lancashire, one trait that unites is their bucolic beauty. The stunning landscapes on and around the Pennines are natural Britain at its rural, rugged best, and provide a perfect backdrop for a scenic cycle ride.

Since opening in September 2010, the Way of the Roses route, which runs between Morecambe and Bridlington, has developed a dedicated fan base among thousands of cyclists. With all the elements of a perfect bike ride – iconic landscapes, a following wind (unless you're unlucky), undulating hills, fantastic scenery, welcoming tea shops and a feeling that you could pedal on forever – it's no wonder it has become a much-loved route. The Way of the Roses offers something for everyone: great for a little jaunt or the full 170 miles; taking it easy and enjoying the scenery, or using it to test yourself.

I'd recommend staying in Morecambe the night before you start your cycle. The sunsets over the Bay provide a stunning prelude to your ride, particularly combined with a night at the tastefully refurbished art deco Midland Hotel. As with other sections of the route, there are a few hilly bits soon after you pass through Lancaster: but who doesn't enjoy the thrill of a downhill ride? It's one of life's true pleasures and costs nothing! Ride highlights begin straight after departure from Morecambe, with fascinating artwork complementing the breathtaking views across the bay to the Lakes. The route also provides a great outlook on the stunning scenes of the Lune Valley, the Forest of Bowland and the Dales.

However, my favourite moment on the route lies six miles outside the town of Settle where an outdoor pursuit paradise provides a kind of natural theme park loved by walkers, mountain bikers and abseilers from across the country.

I am ashamed to say that even though I'm a local boy, some of the places on the route were quite new to me. I must give a big cheer to Sustrans and its partners for opening up this hidden gem of a landscape.

My advice to anyone planning to do the ride is simply: do it! I can't wait for my next trip.

Wayne Hemingway
Sustrans Patron

Acknowledgements

The idea of a new coast2coast cycle route across Lancashire and Yorkshire first surfaced in 2007. From then onwards to the opening of **Way of the Roses** *in September 2010, many people (and organisations) played a part in its creation. The list would be long but, looking back, I'd personally like to give a mention to Alasdair Simpson, Andy Ryland, Dave Stevens, Cathy Hopley, Martyn Bolt, David Gray, Malcolm and Gia Margolis, Martin and Yvonne Weeks, Suzi Bunting (then Williams), Chris Fowler, Paul Roberts, Andy Vose, Ian Burnett, Ann Widnall, Mike Dagley and finally David Hall, Sustrans Regional Director for Yorkshire, who saw fit to host my role during the route's development.*

It took a while for the Way of the Roses name to emerge from much debate. Oddly enough it was a suggestion through Otley Town Council who were very keen to be part of a southern strand which didn't quite happen.

The early success of the route is due in no small part to the efforts of various local authority staff and Sustrans volunteers to keep the route open and well signed.

Last but not least, thanks go to David Barbour at Stirling Surveys, Holly Coupland and Julian Hunt at Sustrans, and our designer Mike Cooper for their parts in producing this guidebook.

Rupert Douglas – June 2013

CONTENTS

Image © Cooper Douglas

Riding from coast-to-coast is an alluringly simple cycle touring proposition, especially here in the narrow North of England where so much outstanding scenery and heritage is packed in between the Irish Sea and North Sea. It's rather like a modern day secular pilgrimage.

Way of the Roses is the most recent addition to the Sustrans family of coast to coast routes, and one that is proving popular with those looking for a road bike friendly route that's achievable over several days.

It's a challenging adventure both in terms of distance and terrain, with the ups and downs of the hilly Forest of Bowland, Yorkshire Dales, Nidderdale and Yorkshire Wolds to negotiate. You are richly rewarded for your efforts as on a bicycle you can experience the variety of beautiful landscapes, and the fascinating history and culture, first hand – not to mention the fresh air, freedom and fun of propelling yourself along well signed quiet roads, country lanes and cycle paths.

The name *Way of the Roses*, with its distinctive signing, derives not so much from the Wars of the Roses (see p14), but from the red and white roses that have come to symbolise the two iconic northern counties of Lancashire and Yorkshire which the route traverses. The two terminus points are set on the promenades at Morecambe and Bridlington, two reviving seaside resorts, which are relatively easy to get to by train.

Cycling is a great way to whet your appetite, and you'll really enjoy the many tempting refreshment stops and tasty regional produce that's never too far away. Starting at the western end is usually best to take advantage of our prevailing south westerly winds.

Finally, build a little slack into your schedule. Savour the views, exchange a few words with friendly locals, or maybe visit one of the many places of interest along the way.

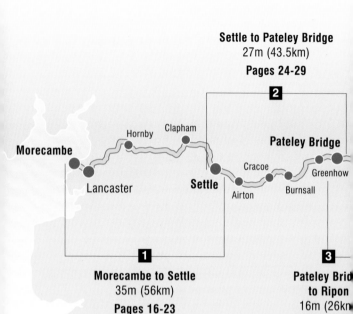

Settle to Pateley Bridge
27m (43.5km)
Pages 24-29

2

Hornby
Clapham

Pateley Bridge

Morecambe

Cracoe
Greenhow

Lancaster

Settle

Airton
Burnsall

1

3

Morecambe to Settle
35m (56km)
Pages 16-23

Pateley Brid
to Ripon
16m (26kn

Pages 30-3

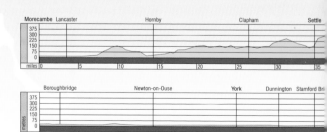

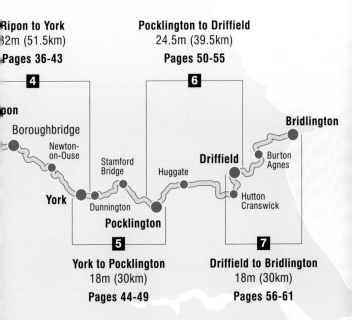

Ripon to York
32m (51.5km)
Pages 36-43

4

pon

Boroughbridge

Newton-
on-Ouse

Stamford
Bridge

York

Dunnington

Pocklington to Driffield
24.5m (39.5km)
Pages 50-55

6

Huggate

Driffield

Bridlington

Burton
Agnes

Hutton
Cranswick

Pocklington

5

York to Pocklington
18m (30km)

Pages 44-49

7

Driffield to Bridlington
18m (30km)

Pages 56-61

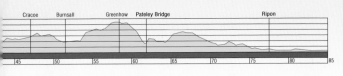

Cracoe Burnsall Greenhow Pateley Bridge Ripon

45 50 55 60 65 70 75 80 85

on Huggate Hutton Cranswick Driffield Burton Agnes Bridlington

130 135 140 145 150 155 160 165 170

Finding your way

This guidebook has been written to accompany the Sustrans Way of the Roses cycle route map, which you are recommended to take with you. Despite the best efforts of Sustrans and its partners to keep the route easy to follow, signs do get moved and go missing. You may also have to travel off the route to find accommodation or a bike shop for example, or in the event of a diversion. News about temporary and permanent changes to the route appear on the official website *www.wayoftheroses.info*.

Where to stay

There's a variety of accommodation along the route, mostly bed & breakfast, but also hostels, bunkhouse barns and camp sites. Many of these are featured on the official *wayoftheroses.info* website. A selection of mainly cyclist friendly B&Bs (with cycle storage and either offering food or with places to eat nearby), are shown at the end of each section of the guidebook.

The YHA has hostels at Malham (see page 27) and in York (see page 41), where private rooms as well as dormitories are available – call *0800 0191 700* or visit *www.yha.org.uk*

These and other hostels *(www.independenthostelguide.co.uk)*, together with camping / bunkhouse barns, are marked on the Way of the Roses map.

Camping sites are also marked on the map. Facilities do vary so try and check before you arrive. Some sites are Camping & Caravanning Club certified – *www.campingandcaravanningclub.co.uk*

Tourist Information Centres will help you find accommodation, and are shown both on the map and in each section of this guidebook. For the Lancashire section of the route *www.visitlancashire.com* has information about places to stay, for the Yorkshire section of the route try *www.yorkshire.com*

Look out for accommodation displaying the Cyclists Welcome logo. These businesses have been inspected and assessed by Visit England as providing extra facilities and services for cycling guests.

Finding food & drink

Many of the shops, cafes, tearooms, pubs, and hotels that are on or close to the route are shown on the map, and there's a food & drink page on the *wayoftheroses.info* website site to check

It's advisable to start each day with your water bottles full to keep you hydrated, and with some nutritious snacks to hand. Flapjacks are a popular choice because they're easy to eat and provide both quickfire and slower burn carbohydrates, meaning you won't get a sugar rush followed by a swift drop off in energy. Bananas come nicely packed in their own wrapper, are easy to eat and contain (among other things) high levels of potassium which is necessary for good nerve and muscle function as well as for maintaining a healthy balance of fluids in the body. The potassium in bananas can help prevent muscle cramps after exercise. You will have your own favourites, but on a long day's ride 'little and often' is a good adage to follow.

Bike accessories, repairs & spares

A bell is a must for any cyclist as it lets you warn pedestrians of your approach, and Way of the Roses has several traffic free shared use sections.

For a multi-day ride on Way of the Roses (and assuming your bike is made for a rack), it's best to carry your kit in panniers rather than a rucksack, as rucksacks can make you hot and sweaty and strain your back. A bar bag keeps your map, camera, snacks etc within easy reach. A lightweight bike lock and a bike pump are also recommended, as are bike lights (with spare batteries) just in case you end up riding in the dark.

Setting off with your bike in tip top condition means you'll enjoy the ride more and are less likely to need repairs en route. Make sure the tyres are pumped up and the seat and handlebars are set

to the right position. It's crucial to check your brakes to ensure you can control your speed on numerous steep descents (with the added weight of your panniers). Your chain should be clean and lubricated to help with smooth gear changing on the ascents, and wheel quick releases should be in the closed position.

Cycle shops are shown on the Way of the Roses map and mentioned at the end of each section of this guidebook. However, you could easily get a puncture far from one of them so you need to know how to deal with it. It's simplest just to replace the inner tube and repair the punctured tube later. So take at least one spare tube, tyre levers and a puncture repair kit with you, usually carried in a seat pack under the saddle or in your panniers. A multi-tool is also recommended for a range of adjustments and bolt tightening.

What to wear and what else to take

You shouldn't need to invest in a lot of specialist clothing or footwear to enjoy Way of the Roses. Wear thin layers which you can easily add or remove as you go, and choose breathable fabrics that are quick-drying. A full set of waterproofs is essential, and warm layers are a good idea if you are planning long days and will be out early morning and into the evening, even in summer as the temperature can vary quite dramatically. As well as fingerless padded mitts or gloves and a hat, consider overshoes (your extremities are more exposed when cycling), and remember a reflective top layer for staying visible at night. A peaked hat/helmet, suncream and sunglasses will help when riding in bright sunlight, and padded shorts will make your ride a lot more comfortable.

Wearing a helmet is not compulsory in England so the decision is ultimately a question of individual choice. Although helmets can't prevent accidents from happening they can protect you if they do occur and are especially recommended for young children.

Above all, only take what you're likely to use and keep the weight to a minimum – as soon as you start the first climb you'll be glad you did.

Support services

If you'd prefer not to carry your own kit, there are baggage transfer services, and the option of hiring a bike to do the whole route. Details of these operators and those offering self-guided and guided cycling holidays are on the website *wayoftheroses.info*.

Bikes on trains

It's much easier to catch a train to the start of the route and take another from the end to get you home (as opposed to having to return to collect your car). Services for both Morecambe (from Lancaster) and Bridlington are operated by Northern Rail who are generally pretty good at letting you on with your bike without a reservation. Space is allocated on a first come, first served basis, and strictly speaking they can only carry a maximum of two bikes per train but frequently allow more on.

Problems can arise if you've had to reserve a bike space and buy a ticket for a connecting service with a train from Bridlington, and you can't get your bike (or those of others riding with you) on the train from there. To avoid a last minute panic and risk spoiling your holiday, my advice is not to bank on catching the last possible train from Bridlington.

Bikes are carried free of charge on most UK trains, and there are normally no restrictions on folding bikes. Check carefully though if taking a tandem. *www.tandem-club.org.uk*. For rail travel information call **08457 48 49 50** or visit *www.nationalrail.co.uk*.

Cycling with children

If you are planning on doing some or all of Way of the Roses with kids in tow, you won't be disappointed but do take into consideration that there are some very steep hills and the route is mostly on minor roads, with the occasional section on busier roads.

Image © Glyn Shenhall

Top tips for cycling with children
• Take along snacks, drinks and treats to keep spirits and energy levels up.
• Don't be too ambitious. It's better to take it slow and enjoy it rather than getting tired out.
• Plan each stage around interesting stops and sights along the way. Don't make journey times any longer than children are happy to sit still and play at home.
• Wrap up toddlers. When a young child is on the back of a bike, they won't be generating heat like the person doing all the pedalling and the wind can be cold even during the summer months.
• Ride in a line with the children in the middle of the adults. If there's only one of you, the adult should be at the rear, keeping an eye on all the children in front. Take special care at junctions.
• Carry some sticking plasters and antiseptic wipes – kids are far more likely to fall off and graze arms, hands or knees.

• Children should always wear a securely fitted helmet, whether being carried on your bike or riding their own. Check that it still fits before riding.
• When riding with a child on the back be aware of how the weight affects your bike handling and take care when dismounting.

When to go
Try to avoid the busier bank holidays if you can to make it easier to find single nights in the more visited places like Settle and York, otherwise book well in advance. Although the summer months (generally) provide the balmiest weather and longest days, often the best time to go is spring or autumn when temperatures aren't too high, the route, accommodation and places to visit aren't so busy, and traffic levels can be lower. Some parts of the route are high, exposed and remote so always check weather forecasts beforehand, and be prepared.

Good Cycling Code

Please have a read through this before you set off. It's important that good cycling manners are displayed at all times, especially on narrow and winding country lanes, and shared use paths.

The *Highway Code* does permit you to cycle two abreast, but please be aware of vehicles coming up behind you and move in to a single line to allow them to overtake.

• Always follow the Highway Code
• Cycle within your capabilities; match your speed to the surface, gradient and your skills
• Avoid surprising people: Ring a bell or call out to warn of your approach and acknowledge those who give way to you
• Give way to pedestrians, wheelchair users and horse-riders, leaving them plenty of room, especially when approaching from behind

• Remember that some people are hard of hearing and visually impaired. Don't assume they can see or hear you
• On shared use paths, always be prepared to slow down or stop if necessary. Be particularly careful at junctions, bends, entrances onto paths and any other points where space or visibility are limited
• Keep your bike roadworthy; use lights in poor visibility
• Always carry food, water, a puncture repair kit, a map and waterproofs
• Consider wearing a helmet and high visibility clothing and make sure you are seen
• Follow the Countryside Code and take your litter home with you
• Try to cycle or use public transport to travel to and from the start and finish of your ride.

Travelling Histories Public Art

Whilst **Way of the Roses** is a new route for people to follow over the Pennines between Lancashire and Yorkshire, it comprises a compelling collection of places where natural phenomena and historic movements of people have left their mark. This is the theme for our *Travelling Histories* public art project, artworks for which will start to appear from 2014.

For example, the landscapes at both ends of Way of the Roses have been shaped by running water. At Morecambe this is an ongoing process which changes the landscape every day. At Bridlington, the land retains the memory of movement that occurred at a very precise moment in the past.

Two *Terminus Artworks* are being developed that will start and finish the coast-to-coast journey with powerful evocations of place – they introduce the theme of *'change in landscape'* that the traveller will encounter in many different guises along the route.

Also being developed between the Terminus artworks will be a series of *Passing Place Artworks*. Created through the insight and effort of the communities where they are sited, each of these artworks will be a short diversion from the main cycle route and be designed to take the curious cyclist on an intimate journey of discovery into the stories of some of the many communities along Way of the Roses. Passing Places at Bentham, Pateley Bridge and Stamford Bridge are the first to be developed. More from *www.wayofrosespublicart.org.uk*

Key to maps

══════	On road route
┄┄┄┄┄	Off road sections
──●──4──	Things to see along the route
══════	Main roads/carriageways
══════	Secondary roads
══════	Minor roads
──○──	Motorways/Junctions
──●──	Railways/stations

Grids shown on the route maps represent approximately 4 square kilometres

	0 – 50m
	50 – 100m
	100 – 150m
	150 – 200m
	200 – 250m
	250 – 300m
	300 – 400m
	over 400m
	Settlements
	Rivers/lakes

Wars of the Roses

The Wars of the Roses were not really between Lancashire and Yorkshire, but between the House of York and the House of Lancaster, with battles taking place all over England. The friendly rivalry that now exists between the inhabitants of these two counties stems from these times, but is now no longer so serious.

The route's most direct connection with the wars is in York, where the recent discovery of Richard III's skeleton in Leicester is fuelling great interest.

Richard (1452-1485), the last monarch of the House of York, grew up at Middleham Castle in the Yorkshire Dales and visited York several times during his short reign, staying for three weeks in 1483. He even wished to be buried in York Minster, intending to build an enormous chantry chapel at the Minster where 100 additional chaplains would pray for his soul... a radical ambition as English monarchs were traditionally interred at Westminster Abbey.

York looked to Richard for help at a time of economic decline, and actively championed his short reign. The city sent troops to support his cause, including 80 dispatched to support him after Henry Tudor's invasion. They were too late.

'King Richard, late mercifully reigning over us, was through great treason... piteously slain and murdered, to the great heaviness of this city,' reported the mayor's serjeant of the mace a day after Richard's death at the Battle of Bosworth on 22 August 1485.

Richard's two-year reign signalled the end of the dynastic struggle known as the Wars of the Roses, and is seen by some historians as the last act of the medieval era. His death at Bosworth the last English king to be killed in battle – ushered in the Tudor dynasty beginning with Henry VII.

Shakespeare then helped to make Richard notorious as one of the English language's most memorable villains. While he remains for many historians the prime suspect in the death of his nephews – the Princes in the Tower – the skeleton's discovery has provided a golden opportunity for those seeking to restore his reputation.

The Richard III Museum in York (just off the route on Goodramgate at Monk Bar, on the city walls) was developed in honour of a King many felt had been unjustly maligned by historians, and is well worth a visit. Admission half price for Sustrans staff, supporters and volunteers. *www.richardiiimuseum.co.uk*

The *www.wars-of-the-roses.com* website is a good source of more information.

The National Cycle Network

ustrans and the National Cycle etwork

ustrans is a leading UK charity behind any groundbreaking projects including 'ay of the Roses and the National Cycle etwork.

he Network provides over 14,000 miles f routes across the UK and includes cenic traffic-free paths, quiet roads and hemed long-distance routes. Sustrans eeds to spend over £1 million a year n route maintenance alone so please onsider supporting Sustrans if you enjoy sing the National Cycle Network and vant it to keep on growing.

Vhat's your favourite mile?

ou can sponsor your favourite mile on 'ay of the Roses or any route on the etwork.

Go to *www.sustrans.org.uk/mymile* to pick your mile and sponsor it for for just £30 a year. You can upload a photo and the reason why you love your mile. As a sponsor you'll receive a thank you pack including an exclusive Sponsor a mile certificate and reflective bike sticker. You'll also receive email updates giving you details of the latest news and events on the Network.

For more information about this and other ways you can support Sustrans please visit *www.sustrans.org.uk* or call *0845 838 0651*

Sponsor your favourite mile on Way of the Roses at **www.sustrans.org.uk/mymile**

How far: 35 miles (56km)

How tough: 1669ft (509m) of climb.
Flat and traffic free to Crook o'Lune, then rolling
roads to Settle with several short steep climbs.

INFORMATION CENTRES

Morecambe: 01524 582808
across from the Midland Hotel
Lancaster: 01524 582394 near
the Castle on Meeting House Lane
Settle: 01729 825192
in the Market Place Town Hall

Morecambe to Settle

Morecambe Bay's broad open expanse, with Lakeland fells rising from its northern edge, makes a fine setting from which to begin your journey from the Irish Sea to the North Sea. The tide goes out a long way here, so you may have to forgo the customary wheel dip.

Crossing the sands of Morecambe Bay has historically been so dangerous because of the racing tides, quicksand and shifting channels) that the post of Queen's Guide to the Sands was created to lead travellers safely across. This post has been held by Cedric Robinson since 1963. Laurel 'brobs' (branches) pressed into the sand are traditionally used to mark the route which will then be erased by the next incoming tide.

Guided walks across the Bay are organised during the summer months (Morecambe Visitor Information Centre has details), so it's well worth trying to coincide your ride with one of them, and also give yourself a little more time to seek out the local delicacy, potted shrimps,

and smile at the statue to Eric Morecambe, Morecambe's most famous son.

Should tide times and weather conditions preclude such a walk, you can just cycle along the promenade and enjoy the artworks, teeming bird life and, quite possibly, a stunning sunset.

The western end of the route, known as The Bastion, is just south of the Stone Jetty and the Art Deco Midland Hotel. The Way of the Roses sign points you across the promenade and through the gap in the sea defence wall. You are quickly onto the pencil straight path that eases you nicely into the ride, and towards the outline of England's Pennine spine.

Image © Cooper Douglas

The cable-stayed Millennium Bridge gets you and many other cyclists and walkers across the River Lune to the edge of the historic city of Lancaster. Your route continues upstream through the River Lune Millennium Park with its 12 permanent artworks, but a short detour into the city centre is easily made by following the blue National Route 6 signs onto Chapel Street.

Onward, passing under the elegant Lune Aqueduct, and cross the river once more before leaving the riverside path (over the next bridge and half a mile further on is Caton, which has shops, a pub and a pharmacy). A narrow track on the left takes you up to the lovely Crook O'Lune viewpoint. This marks a change in the terrain as having taken to the road the first steep climb is encountered within a mile of pedalling along Park Lane.

From near the Crook O'Lune, the route tracks the northern edge of the Forest of Bowland Area of Outstanding Natural Beauty. Down from

Gressingham hamlet, the medieval Loyne Bridge affords your final crossing of the River Lune for you to then rise out of its valley into this upland landscape that forms part of the Pennines.

After the refreshment stops offered by riverside Hornby and Wray villages, the route finds undulating Mewith Lane and your road out of Lancashire into Yorkshire. The actual line is marked by the unassuming carved parish boundary stone on the bridge over the beck between map mile markers 19 and 20.

Image © Cooper Douglas

Image © Cooper Douglas

Image © Paul Harris

Image © Sam Howard

The Forest of Bowland is a paradise for birdwatchers. The sharp eyed cyclist might spot Little Owls sitting on top of dry stone walls in the morning and evening, or family groups of common buzzards circling overhead. Your elevated position also affords fine views of the Yorkshire Dales as some of the most magnificent examples of carboniferous limestone in Britain, draw ever close.

At the next crossroads you can turn right uphill for the great stone of Fourstones (see page 23), first of several big stones on this ride, or left downhill into High Bentham, a small but well catered market town. Turning left at the Keasden crossroads note 'Yorks WR' in the road sign finial showing how far the old West Riding of Yorkshire (1889-1974) extended from its headquarters in Wakefield.

If the river's not too high, try the underpass under the A65 to enter the ancient and picturesque village of Clapham, your doorway to the Yorkshire Dales National Park. Clapham sits at the base of Ingleborough mountain, one of Yorkshire's 'Three Peaks' (Pen-y-ghent and Whernside being the other two). Clapham lies in the Craven Fault zone, a complex series of geological faults which marks the division of the sandstone rocks of the Bowland area and the distinctive limestone outcrops and scars of the Dales.

The path alongside the A65 (adjacent to a newly constructed dry stone wall) makes it easy to reach Austwick. If staying here overnight, an evening stroll above the village is a must to see the Norber erratics, glacially-transported sandstone boulders from further north in Crummackdale. They were deposited on the limestone when the ice melted about 15,000 years ago. Some of the erratics have protected the limestone beneath them, while the

surrounding surface has slowly been dissolved away. These erratics now rest on upstanding blocks of limestone, known as pedestals, some of which reach 60 metres in height.

From Austwick, the route winds gently upwards between dry stone walls to the rim of the Ribble Valley, where you turn right and head down to the bustling market town of Settle, with the famous Settle – Carlisle Railway on the opposite side of the river.

Image © Dr Neil Clifton

PLACES TO STAY

Morecambe, Lancaster and Settle all offer a choice of overnight accommodation, and there are places to stay in and between villages along the route.

Morecambe
Westleigh 01524 418352
Berkeley 01524 418201
Crown Hotel 01524 831841
Midland Hotel 08458 501 240
High Bentham (near)
Halsteads Barn Country B&B
015242 62641
Clapham
New Inn 015242 51203
Clapham Bunkhouse 01524 251144
(also has a bar and cafe)
Austwick
The Traddock 015242 51224

Giggleswick
Valleymead Guest House
01729 822386
Harts Head Inn 01729 822086
Settle
Settle Lodge B&B 01729 823258
The Lion 01729 822203

BIKE SHOPS & REPAIRS

Lancaster
The Edge Cycleworks (01524 840800) is just off the riverside as you follow the cycle route signs for Lancaster city centre. After Morecambe and Lancaster, the next cycle shop is 30 miles away...
Settle
Three Peaks Cycles (01729 824232) in the Market Place

THINGS TO SEE

1 Eric Morecambe statue ▲
A slightly larger than life-sized statue depicting the taller of the comedy duo, who took his stage name from his home town. Worth seeing at night with superb lighting effects.

2 Lancaster Castle and Museums ▲
All located in and around the historic city centre. Guided tours at the Castle, the Cit Museum is free, and the riverside Maritime Museum has a cafe (open all year).

3 Lune Aqueduct ▼
Designed by John Rennie to carry the Lancaster Canal over the river. Completed in 1797, its five arches are built on huge tree trunks sourced from what is now Lithuania. Worth walking up for the views.

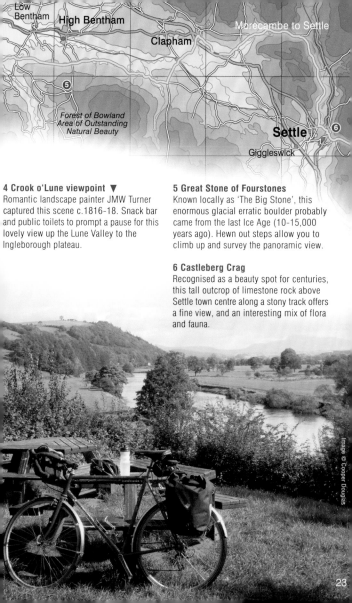

Low Bentham

High Bentham

Clapham

Settle

Giggleswick

Forest of Bowland
Area of Outstanding
Natural Beauty

4 Crook o'Lune viewpoint ▼

Romantic landscape painter JMW Turner captured this scene c.1816-18. Snack bar and public toilets to prompt a pause for this lovely view up the Lune Valley to the Ingleborough plateau.

5 Great Stone of Fourstones

Known locally as 'The Big Stone', this enormous glacial erratic boulder probably came from the last Ice Age (10-15,000 years ago). Hewn out steps allow you to climb up and survey the panoramic view.

6 Castleberg Crag

Recognised as a beauty spot for centuries, this tall outcrop of limestone rock above Settle town centre along a stony track offers a fine view, and an interesting mix of flora and fauna.

Image © Cooper Douglas

How far: 27 miles (43.5km)

How tough: 2066ft (630m) of climb.
Hilly all the way, with two very steep climbs and
one very steep descent, and all on road.

INFORMATION CENTRES

Settle: 01729 825192
in the Market Place Town Hall
Grassington: 01756 751690
on the Hebden Road
Pateley Bridge: 0845 389 0179
up the High Street

Image © Sustrans

Settle to Pateley Bridge

This is the toughest part of the route, taking you up to and over its highest point. The climb out of Settle up High Hill Lane is the hardest of the whole route (and even includes a nice little cobblestone section at the start).

If you've stayed in Settle and had a full Yorkshire breakfast, then you might want to have a ride round on the relative flat before tackling the climb. If you've the gears and strength, and packed light enough to pedal to the top then bravo, but there's no harm in pushing your bike and enjoying the unfolding views of the rugged limestone scenery.

You'll have time to get your breath back on the gradual descent to Airton, and if refreshment is called for, turn left at the T-junction for the farm shop and tea room at Town End Farm and enjoy the lovely view of Malham Cove. Originally a Quaker village, you can now stay in the meeting house, and there's a squatter's cottage on the village green.

A Swaledale ram's head on the signs indicates that since your approach to Clapham, we have been using a section of the 130 mile (209km) Yorkshire Dales Cycleway. This takes us all the way to Appletreewick. Cracoe, which has a cafe and a farm shop tearoom, is where you could leave the route if staying in Grassington (keeping on the busier B road), or carry on to Thorpe and head in from there. Take care when turning right onto the lovely narrow lane that pitches

you up and down, flanked by the characteristic dry stone walls that are such a feature of the Dales. Keep an eye out for sparrowhawks with their dashing flight in pursuit of smaller birds.

Dropping into Wharfedale you descend into the stunningly picturesque villages of Burnsall, and then Appletreewick. Both have wild swimming spots to tempt you. To get down to the River Wharfe in Appletreewick, follow the track opposite the New Inn, as this is probably the easiest with a bicycle.

On the bend, just after the turn for Bolton Abbey, Skyreholme Lane leads off to Parcevall Hall Gardens and the green lane over Pock Stones Moor (refer to the map for onward routing). The route then rears sharply to the left and continues to rise up on to the wilder and grittier moorlands that mark the boundary between the Yorkshire Dales National Park and the Nidderdale Area of Outstanding Natural Beauty (AONB). This is a working landscape that has been shaped by centuries of human activity.

A final kick brings you up to Stump Cross Caverns, a designated site of special scientific interest. Between here and the former lead mining village of Greenhow you're on the highest bit of the route topping out at 1312ft (404m). Although it's not quite all downhill from here to your final destination, you have now broken the back of the biggest climbs.

With a following wind pushing you along you soon start to gather speed, passing the turn to the Coldstones Cut artwork. Greenhow Hill gets six out of ten in Simon Warren's 100 Greatest Cycling

Climbs so you'll appreciate the concentration required to safely descend its four distinct and winding sections, with gradients up to 18%, over almost 2.5 miles. There's information specifically about this challenge on the official website.

You'll still be feathering your brakes as you freewheel into Pateley Bridge (just Pateley to locals), a charming little market town. If you've time, follow the River Nidd upstream to see more of the majestic dale that is the central feature of this AONB.

Alternative route via Malham Tarn

To immerse yourself fully in a more remote and rugged landscape, there's the option of a detour via Malham Tarn. Look at the Way of the Roses map to see a section of the Yorkshire Dales Cycleway heading upwards from Stainforth (north of Settle). If you've come into Settle, retrace the route back to Little Stainforth and turn right.

It's a severe ascent up to Malham Tarn but, in decent weather, it's well worth it to

PLACES TO STAY

Grassington (just over 2 miles off the route after Cracoe) and Pateley Bridge offer a choice of overnight accommodation, and there are places to stay in and around villages along the route.

Airton
Lindon Guest House 01729 830418
Malham
YHA hostel 0845 371 9529 is a mile north of the route from Airton
Cracoe
Brookside Cottage 01756 730338
Devonshire Arms 01756 730237
Grassington
Black Horse Hotel 01756 752770
Burnsall
Wharfe View Farmhouse B&B
01756 720643
Devonshire Fell 01756 729000
Burnsall Village Hall 01756 720680
is good for groups
Appletreewick
New Inn 01756 720252
Fancarl House 01756 752753
Pateley Bridge
Lindale Guest House 01423 712657
Talbot Hotel 01423 711597
Harefield Hall 01423 715840

enjoy this unique area of limestone pavements, upland hill farms and flower-rich hay meadows, home to a unique community of rare plants and animals.

Sticking to the road only gives you the briefest glimpse of the glacial tarn itself (England's highest lake), so, if time permits, turn left following the signs for the Malham Tarn Field Studies Centre, then right onto the private road (and part rough track) that takes you around the tarn and back onto the road.

All of this area is managed by The National Trust, and in the field on your right just past their offices, summertime camping and some simple refreshments are being developed. It's probably best to check before you set off by calling the estate office on 01729 830416 or by enquiring at Settle Tourist Information Centre.

Carry straight on where the track joins the road and descend carefully down to pretty Malham village with pubs, cafes and a shop. As you enter the village you can turn right and pedal up a short way for a view of Malham Cove itself. Malham is understandably a popular spot so be mindful of the traffic making its way up the dale as you head down through Kirkby Malham to rejoin the route at Airton.

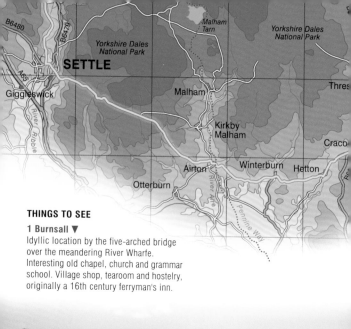

THINGS TO SEE

1 Burnsall ▼

Idyllic location by the five-arched bridge
over the meandering River Wharfe.
Interesting old chapel, church and grammar
school. Village shop, tearoom and hostelry,
originally a 16th century ferryman's inn.

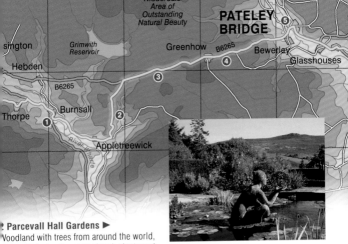

2 Parcevall Hall Gardens ▶

Woodland with trees from around the world, and south facing terraces of rock plants and roses. Free admission to tea room to relax and enjoy some spectacular views of Wharfedale (open Apr to Sep).

3 Stump Cross Caverns

A chance to go underground to see caves which began forming millions of years ago when the Yorkshire Dales lay under an ocean. Free admission to film show and tearoom (from Mar to Nov).

BIKE SHOPS & REPAIRS

Pateley Bridge

There isn't a cycle shop in Pateley Bridge itself, but just over a mile further along the B6165 from Wilsill (and your left turn to Brimham Rocks), is **Stif Cycles** (01423 780738): turn right into the New York Mills Industrial Estate.

Appletreewick

At the top of the New Inn car park is John Pitcher's **Mountain Bike Livery** where tools are at hand to help with running repairs in the dry (open most days).

4 Coldstones Cut ▲

The biggest and highest piece of public artwork in Yorkshire. Ancient stone blocks combine with a contemporary streetscape and platforms to see the limestone quarrying and survey surrounding Nidderdale. Easier to leave your bikes by the gateway to the path leading up to it than in the car park .

5 Nidderdale Museum

Houses a large indoor collection illustrating all aspects of life in Nidderdale, including an original cobbler's shop, a Victorian parlour, general store and school room. Small admission charge and toilets (open Easter to Oct).

How far: 16 miles (26km)

How tough: 918ft (280m) of climb. A steep pull up to Brimham rocks then moderating country lanes nearer to Ripon.

INFORMATION CENTRES

Pateley Bridge: 01423 711147
8 High Street
Ripon: 01765 604625
Minster Road (opposite the cathedral)

Pateley Bridge to Ripon

Hopefully refreshed, it's up Pateley's narrow High Street and a little further down Nidderdale, to the last steep, sustained climb of the whole route. The crossroads at the top is a good place to catch your breath and on a clear day, drink in the wonderful and vast view across the Vale of York; the lower lying Yorkshire Wolds hills often discernible in the distance (it's the Howardian Hills, Hambleton Hills and then Cleveland Hills you can also see as you scan northwards).

Next you're amongst the curious shapes of Brimham's balancing rocks. You can cycle along the track, beyond the car parks, to the visitor centre and other facilities to see and find out more. It's a good place for a scramble and to enjoy a picnic bought from the tempting food shops in Pateley. Or, you may prefer to sit atop a rock in quiet contemplation – if so, you might witness a flying and singing display from lapwing, skylarks or curlews, depending on the time of year.

The landscape gradually becomes more pastoral, dry stone walls giving way to hedgerows, as you follow country lanes by woodland and fields down to the River Skell for a last little pull up into Fountains Abbey & Studley Royal. Here, at the only World Heritage Site on the route, there is a cycle friendly visitor centre and restaurant just off the first roundabout. Otherwise it's through the gate and onto the road through the medieval deer park, renowned as a great place for photography. If you pass through in rutting season you may be able to capture tangling antlers from the mature stags but, deer (fallow, sika and red) are notoriously shy so you'll be very lucky. If you're in a hurry, the ancient oaks and sweet chestnuts are much more ready to pose and can be equally impressive. Shot taken, the towers of Ripon Cathedral beckon in the distance.

Image © Cooper Douglas

Ripon is just a few miles further on and rather a gem of a small Yorkshire town. Perhaps what helps to set it apart is that for 1000 years it administered its own justice and policed its own streets. To this day, at 9 o'clock each evening, the Hornblower sets the night watch at the four corners of the obelisk in the Market Square.

Catching this atmospheric nightly occurrence, plus the Cathedral, local museums and the opportunity to spend more time at Fountains Abbey, all add to the attractiveness of Ripon and make it an ideal place to break your journey and stay an extra night.

Another possibility is a panniers-free ride up to Masham (about 11 miles via Kirkby Malzeard and Grewelthorpe), a smaller edge of Dales market town that's uniquely home to two of Yorkshire's most well known ales – Black Sheep and Theakston's. Both breweries have excellent visitor centres and tours.

PLACES TO STAY

There's a choice of overnight accommodation in and around Ripon.

Bishop Thornton
Dukes Place Courtyard 01765 620229
Studley Roger
Jelley Legs 01765 603506
Ripon
Box Tree Cottages 01765 698006
Lavender House 01765 505469
The Old Deanery 01765 600003

BIKE SHOPS & REPAIRS

Ripon
Moonglu (01765 601106) on Blossomgate is the only cycle shop before Boroughbridge

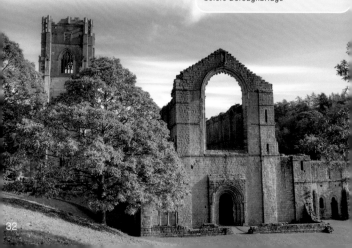

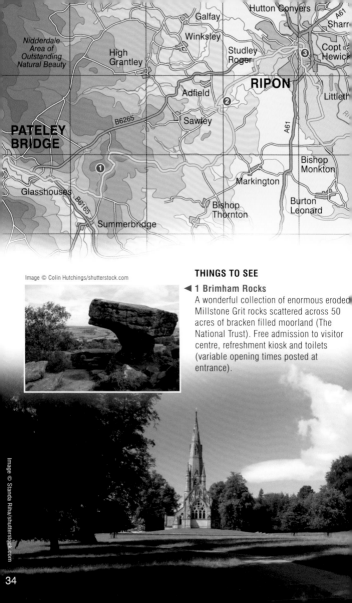

Image © Colin Hutchings/shutterstock.com

THINGS TO SEE

◀ **1 Brimham Rocks**
A wonderful collection of enormous eroded Millstone Grit rocks scattered across 50 acres of bracken filled moorland (The National Trust). Free admission to visitor centre, refreshment kiosk and toilets (variable opening times posted at entrance).

◀ 3 Ripon Cathedral
The cathedral is an impressive building dating from 672 with an ancient Saxon crypt and medieval woodcarvings on the choir stalls. Free admission.

3 Ripon Museums
Spread over three sites in the city centre, The Yorkshire Law & Order Museums tell the unique story of the Liberty Courthouse, Prison and Victorian Workhouse. Admissions charged (open Feb to Nov).

3 Hornblower ▼
The red-coated Hornblower sets the night watch and tells a story every night at 9 o'clock, all year round by the obelisk in the Market Square.

Fountains Abbey & Studley Royal
Britain's largest monastic ruin and most complete 12th-century Cistercian abbey (and only surviving corn mill), together with one of the best examples of a Georgian water garden, all set in 800 acres of beautiful countryside (National Trust). Free admission to visitor centre and restaurant, with ample cycle parking, and a lakeside tearoom (open all year).

Image © Cooper Douglas

How far: 32 miles (51.5km)

How tough: 66ft (20m) of climb.
Largely flat country lanes leading to the riverside
path into York.

INFORMATION CENTRES

Ripon: 01765 604625
Minster Road (opposite the
cathedral)
York: 01262 673374
1 Museum Street (approx 300
yards south from the Minster)

Image © www.visityork.org

Ripon to York

South-eastwards from Ripon the cycling becomes much easier as you cross the low lying Vale of York to bridge the gap between the Pennines and the Yorkshire Wolds. It's a welcome rest for your legs and time to enjoy a steadier cadence. It's noticeable on this section that the dry stone walls, grit, sandstone and other distinctive architecture of the Yorkshire Dales have given way to red brick and pan-tile roofs that reflect the change in geology and landscape.

The route loosely follows the River Ure through charming villages to the small town of Boroughbridge, which roughly marks the halfway point on your journey.

The entrance to Boroughbridge is marked by the prehistoric standing stones known as Devils Arrows on either side of the road just after the A1(M) underpass and roundabout.

Image © stone-circles.org.uk

Image © Cooper Douglas

Image © Sam Howard

Half a mile further along the route is Aldborough, now a village but once the principal town in the area during the Roman period. After the Norman Conquest the crossing of Dere Street (the Roman Road heading to the North from York) over the Ure was diverted from just north of Aldborough to its present position in Boroughbridge. A new town grew up around this crossing and, whilst the Old Town became known as the 'Ald-Borough' (hence Aldborough), the New Town became 'New Borough on t'Brigg' (Brigg being Bridge), which naturally became 'Borough on t'Brigg' and finally Boroughbridge.

It's now the River Ouse that the route keeps company with. Following any prolonged period of rainfall, the Ouse gathers more water from other parts of the Dales, and is therefore prone to flooding. Refer to the map and seek local knowledge if you need to find an alternative route. The river is crossed using the Aldwark toll bridge, one of the few in the country that are privately owned. Cyclists are requested to stop but happily are allowed to cross for free.

The final highlight before reaching York is Beningborough Hall & Gardens. If you arrive after closing time, don't be put off by the seemingly gated entrance, the chain is long enough for you to get through and continue through the parkland. There's also a very nice farm shop cafe just past the Hall if you decide not to stop there.

The impressive medieval city of York now beckons and thankfully a traffic free riverside route is provided off Stripes Lane just past Overton hamlet. From under Scarborough Railway Bridge (one of nine bridges across the Ouse within the city), the route finds the road again and takes you through Bootham Bar gatehouse. Pedal on with care along the narrow and usually pedestrian filled street to emerge right by the towers of the Minster, the second largest gothic cathedral in Northern Europe.

As you pass by the south transept entrance look up to the Rose Window which features red and white Tudor roses commemorating the marriage of Henry Tudor (England's Lancastrian king) and Elizabeth of York in

1486, and marking the end of the Wars of the Roses. There are some separate red roses but no wholly white roses.

There's so much to see and do in York, that it greatly recommends itself as a place to stay over, or at least spend part of the day, especially as it's one of Britain's most cycle friendly places.

There's also a lot be said for getting off your bike and stretching your legs along the 2.5 miles of York's medieval city walls, the most complete in England. You can access them from the Cycle Hub Station down by Lendal Bridge, where you can park your bike indoors for a small fee, and at the Richard III Museum at Monk Bar, where you can find out a bit more about the Wars of the Roses (see page 14).

PLACES TO STAY

There are a handful of places to stay in Boroughbridge, and plenty of choice in the York area.

Roecliffe
Crown Inn 01423 322300
Boroughbridge
Lock House 01423 324970
Crown Hotel 01423 322328
York
The Bloomsbury 01904 634031
Bay Horse 01904 541926
Cumbria House 01904 636817
YHA Hostel 0845 371 9529
just off the route by Clifton Bridge
Racecourse Centre 01904 620911
(ext 284) for groups on a budget
Dunnington
The Windmill 01904 481898

BIKE SHOPS & REPAIRS

Boroughbridge
Karbitz (01423 324085) on High Street do cycle repairs, and there are plenty of cycle shops in York.
Cycle Heaven have shops at the railway station (01904 622701) and on Bishopthorpe Road (01904 636578).
Halfords (01904 61184) is on Foss Islands Road. There's a York Cycle Route Map showing the location of these and other cycle shops, and indicating which offer cycle hire.
York
Hub Station (01904 733789) on the south bank of the river by Lendal Bridge, provides secure bike storage during the day as well as servicing and repairs. (Run by the Bike Rescue Project.)

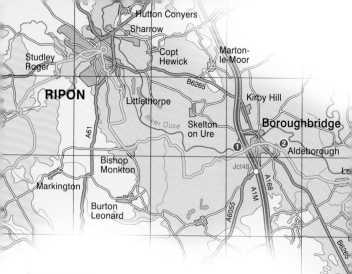

PLACES TO SEE

1 Devils Arrows

Three huge prehistoric standing stones. The stone partially hidden under trees in its own fenced enclosure on the south side of the road stands nearly 7 metres tall, making it the second tallest standing stone in Britain, and only beaten by the mighty 8 metre monolith at Rudston (just off the route near Bridlington).

2 Aldborough Roman Site

Aldborough was the 'capital' of the Romanised Brigantes, the largest Iron Age tribe in Britain. There is a museum, two superb Roman mosaic pavements, and a section of the original town wall (English Heritage). Admission charge, small shop, toilets (open weekends and bank holidays April to September).

3 Beningborough Hall & Gardens

An 18th-century house with 120 importan English portraits from the 17th and 18th centuries on loan from the National Portrai Gallery (National Trust). Free audio tour, working walled garden and plenty for kids to do. Admission charge (refreshment only voucher for cyclists), kiosk, restaurant, toilets (open all year).

Image © www.visityork.org

Image © www.visityork.org

York Minster

Begun during the time of Archbishop Walter le Gray in 1220, the Minster took 250 years to complete. Almost 4000 people can fit in for a service and the Great East Window is one of the largest areas of medieval stained glass anywhere in the world. Interactive displays in the underground chambers, and 275 narrow steps to the top of the Central Tower. Admission charge, toilets (open all year). The **Treasurer's House** (National Trust) is just behind it with a tearoom.

5 National Railway Museum ▲

The largest railway museum in the world, with over 100 locomotives and all manner of railway paraphernalia, art, film and much more. Free entry (donations encouraged), restaurant, cafe, toilets (open all year).

Linton-on-Ouse

Newton-on-Ouse

③

River Nidd

River Ouse

Shipton

Haxby

A19

A1237

Skelton

A64

Nether Poppleton

YORK

A59

B1224

④ ⑦

Osbaldwick

⑤ ⑥

Acomb

Heslington

A1237

Fulford

A64

Bishopthorpe

6 Jorvik

Journey in time capsules through the Viking-age city of Jorvik, reconstructed on the 1000 year old site discovered by York Archaeological Trust during their five year dig at Coppergate. Admission charge, open all year.

7 Richard III Museum

Situated in York's tallest and most impressive medieval gatehouse (Monk Bar), still has a working portcullis. Admission charge (Sustrans staff, supporters and volunteers half price) open all year.

How far: 18 miles (30km)

How tough: 98ft (30m) of climb
Flat to very gently undulating on shared paths
and quiet roads.

INFORMATION CENTRES

York: 01262 673374
1 Museum Street (Approx 300
yards south from the Minster)

Image © Glyn Shentall

The easier cycling continues as you leave your way out of York to the edge of the Yorkshire Wolds. Take your time going by the Minster and take care not to miss the right turn into Aldwark (just before Monk Bar) as it's often crowded with pedestrians, vehicles and other cyclists.

Keep following the signs to cross the relatively new traffic-free bridge over the River Foss and by Morrisons supermarket to reach the Foss Island railway path to Murton.

Leaving Murton you pass the Yorkshire Museum of Farming which has a cafe. Although sandwiched between two main roads, Dunnington village feels like you're

back in the countryside again, and the mile of unsurfaced route past Hagg Wood definitely has a rustic feel to it.

A quiet private road leads to another traffic-free section, this time well surfaced, first through a copse and then across the viaduct (originally carrying the York – Beverley railway line) and over the River Derwent running through Stamford Bridge.

Image © Sam Howard

45

Image © Cooper Douglas

There has been a river crossing just here since at least Roman times. There was a bridge at or near the village in the 11th century, which is referred to in accounts of the landmark battle of 1066 which took place on 25th September and marked the end of the Viking era in Britain. There is a small monument on the opposite side of the main road in the centre of the village (in front of the old corn mill). This and the cafe make a worthwhile little detour.

Three days after the battle, on 28 September, the Normans under William the Conqueror landed on the south coast of England. King Harold had to rush his battered, weary army south to meet the new invasion. Less than three weeks after Stamford Bridge, on 14 October, Harold was defeated and killed at the Battle of Hastings, beginning the Norman Conquest of England, and ending the Anglo-Saxon era.

The Vale of York finally gives way to the rolling chalk hills of the Yorkshire Wolds at the pleasant little market town of Pocklington (known locally as 'Pock'). Turn left into the Market Place to find more refreshment stops.

CTC members may be interested to know that cycling champion George Herbert Stancer was born here in 1878, the year in which the Cyclists Touring Club, the national cycling organisation, was formed. He later became its secretary and its president. He was a British record holder tricyclist in the 1890s, and broke the London to Brighton tandem record. He went on to be one of the country's top cycling journalists and administrators and was made an OBE for services to the sport.

Image © Sam Howard

Image © Cooper Douglas

PLACES TO STAY

After Dunnington, bed & breakfast is available at Stamford Bridge and Pocklington.

Stamford Bridge
Birk House Farm 01759 303071
Pocklington
Ashfield Farmhouse 01759 305238
The Feathers Hotel 01759 303155
Kilnwick Percy
Wolds Retreat 01759 305968
Millington
Ramblers Rest 01759 305220

BIKE SHOPS & REPAIRS

Pocklington
CycleLane (01759 306770) tucked away on Clarkes Lane (behind the NatWest Bank) is the only cycle shop between York and Driffield.

THINGS TO SEE

1 Yorkshire Museum of Farming ▶
Charts the history of farm and rural life across the Ridings of Yorkshire. Train rides on the last remaining section of the Derwent Valley Light Railway. Admission charged, cafe and toilets (open Apr–Nov).

Image © Richard Harvey/commons.wikimedia.org

Image © Cooper Douglas

◀ 2 Battle of Stamford Bridge
As well as the village centre monument, there's a plaque bearing a brief account of the 1066 battle at the end of White Rose Drive (on your left as heading out of the village). Very little has been uncovered to confirm its actual location.

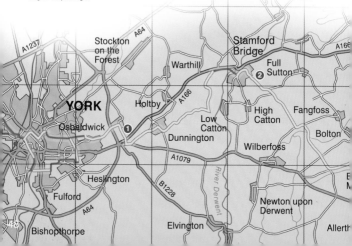

8 Burnby Hall Gardens ▼

Two lakes provide a natural setting for a national collection of hardy water lilies. Small museum about Major Percy Marlborough Stewart - the adventurer and traveller who created them. Admission charged, cafe and toilets (open all year).

Image © Cooper Douglas

Millington

POCKLINGTON

Nunburnholme

How far: 24.5 miles (39.5km)

How tough: 492ft (150m) of climb.
Mostly rolling road which flattens out after
Hutton Cranswick.

INFORMATION CENTRES

There are no information
centres on this section of
the route

Pocklington to Driffield

Shortly out of Pocklington, there's a welcome return to rolling countryside and your rested legs need to start working harder as the road rises past the entrance to the Buddhist centre at Kilnwick Percy Hall, which has a World Peace, whole-food, vegetarian cafe.

You continue climbing steadily onto the Yorkshire Wolds, then it's down and up into picturesque Millington. With both a tearoom and a pub, it's a popular spot with cyclists and walkers (being on the Yorkshire Wolds Way National Trail). From Pocklington you've also been on the circular Yorkshire Wolds Cycle Route.

Continuing along the narrow lanes and down a little alpine-like switch back section takes you to delightful Millington Dale,

a classic Wolds dry valley formed by glacial meltwater. Little surface water stands on the free draining chalkland, and it's uncommon to see streams such as the one feeding the pond on your right although there are numerous springs.

YORKSHIRE WOLDS
Driffield 19

The wooden posts you pass spell out 'GAIT IN WOLDS' - common grazing land was divided into Gaits before the Pastures became enclosed by fencing. The Gaits were looked after by the Pasture Master and were rented to local farmers, each gait being enough grazing for six sheep or four ewes with lambs. Nowadays you're as likely to see hardy Highland Cattle here as sheep, as they are naturally suited to foraging all year round on the hilly Wolds.

Image © Cooper Douglas

You may well have already spotted common buzzards further back on the route, (with their distinctive mewing sound) but keep an eye out here for red kites, hovering kestrels, barrel-chested barn owls, and brown hares.

After a final foray into lower gears you break out onto the high Wolds and head down (leaving the Yorkshire Wolds Cycle Route) into Huggate. World renowned artist David Hockney came to work stacking corn on a farm near here as a teenage boy from industrial Bradford. He's quoted as saying *"It made me fall in love with this part of the world, and I cycled all over it. And cycling, you really do realize it's quite hilly. It's not flat at all."*

His interest in this landscape evolved naturally but eventually he was drawn

PLACES TO STAY

There's accommodation in villages along this section and in Driffield itself.

Huggate
Manor House Farm 01377 288368
Southburn
Highfield Farm 01377 227723
Hutton Cranswick
White Horse Inn 01377 270383
Skerne
The Beeches 01377 254073
Driffield
The Red Lion 01377 255907

BIKE SHOPS & REPAIRS

Driffield
Bells Cycles (01377 253070) (motorcycles as well as bikes), is near Lidl supermarket (turn left at the top of the main street by the clock, then first right).

Image © Cooper Douglas

to painting it, culminating in his hugely popular *A Bigger Picture* exhibition for the Royal Academy of Arts in London early in 2012.

His vivid pictures encourage us to look harder to appreciate the more subtle beauty of the Yorkshire Wolds compared to that of the more obvious appeal of the other upland areas we've cycled through - whatever the season. Woldgate in particular, has inspired much of his recent work and you'll be cycling right along it later as you approach Bridlington, where the artist has a home.

Most likely with the wind at your back, you'll sail along under the big skies the Wolds are noted for and with minimal effort enjoy the steady descent through pleasant villages – and as you reach Hutton Cranswick, look right for the garden centre cafe or, left for the farm shop – and onward to Driffield market town.

If you're looking for a short cut, turn right in Skerne village and go via Wansford (crossing the lovely chalk stream that is the River Hull and the Driffield Navigation canal) to rejoin the route south of Nafferton.

Image © Paul Moon

THINGS TO SEE

◀ **1 Millington Woods**
Beautiful ash woodland in Lily Dale dating back to 1086, with a variety of flowers and butterflies in the summer months. Another good spot for a picnic if you've stocked up on supplies in Pocklington.

2 Driffield Riverhead ▲
The northern (and canal) end
of the 11 mile Driffield
Navigation. Opened in 1770,
it carried agricultural produce
south to the Humber, and coal
upstream into the villages
along its route via the River
Hull. Tearoom looking down
the waterway.

Image © hullvalley.blogspot.com

How far: 18 miles (30km)

How tough: 328ft (100m) of climb.
Flattish lanes apart from rolling Woldgate. Several traffic-free sections. Busier roads and six level crossings lead to Bridlington promenade finish.

INFORMATION CENTRES

Bridlington: 01262 673474 on Prince Street near the harbour

Image © Burton Agnes Hall

Driffield to Bridlington

From the riverhead, the route finds the verge path alongside the old Bridlington Road leading out of Driffield and skirting the edge of the Yorkshire Wolds to Nafferton, a conservation village thanks to its 18th century houses. Remember to turn left onto Coppergate at The Mere, which used to supply several water mills on its south east bank. All Saints' Church on the right is Norman built with a number of curious medieval monuments inside.

The level crossings are for the Yorkshire Coast railway that runs between Hull and Scarborough (via your final destination). Thanks to there being no through route for motor vehicles, the section after the one leaving Nafferton to Lowthorpe is almost traffic-free and very quiet.

Just before the left turn to Harpham, you can stop at the small low bridge and gaze into the crystal clear water of Kelk Beck,

one of the headwaters of the River Hull which are nationally important as the most northerly chalk stream system in Britain.

Harpham's claim to fame is its Well of St John. St John was born in Harpham and later became the Bishop of York in 705 AD. He's the patron saint of the deaf and dumb throughout the world. The well is on the right as you leave the village, and go through a gate onto another traffic-free lane leading to a level crossing.

Before you rise up back onto the Wolds, the small but rather beautiful Burton Agnes Hall & Gardens are definitely worth a stop, if only to take advantage of the tearoom. The best way in for cyclists isn't directly across at the T junction, but by following the route left and up the lane opposite the Blue Bell as signed, and then turning right along the private road by the gatehouse.

Image © Glyn Shentall

Back on the route and up to the top of the ridge brings you to Woldgate, part of the old Roman Road between York and Bridlington. Coastal sea fret permitting, you'll have your first glimpse of the North Sea and Bridlington Bay.

A detour to see Britain's tallest free standing Neolithic stone at Rudston, probably feels counter intuitive with journey's end beckoning, but it's only a mile from the first left turn down to Rudston, across the Gypsey Race (another chalk stream) and by the church.

As mentioned earlier, Woldgate and its trees have shot to fame as the subject of David Hockney's landscape paintings and, more recently, iPad creations (observed in all four seasons) which formed the main body of work for his Royal Academy exhibition.

The majority of visitors to Bridlington's many seaside attractions probably don't get to visit its Georgian Old Town, but it makes a pleasant introduction to this coastal resort.

Past the Priory Church and Bayle Museum (on the site of an Augustinian priory founded in 1113), the route does seem to be taking you away from where you think you should be heading, but press on and soon enough a view of the sea is neatly framed by the arch of the railway bridge over Lime Kiln Lane. You're soon rolling onto the wide promenade with a fine view of the white chalk cliffs of Flamborough Head. The 'Welcome to Bridlington' board by the slipway marks the eastern end of the route, and the conclusion of your personal pilgrimage from the Irish Sea coast at Morecambe.

Congratulations! Ice cream and fish and chips will never have tasted so good.

you've time to linger, cycle back along the promenade and onto the cliff path (shared with the land train) up to Sewerby Hall to savour some more views out to sea. Following the blue cycle route signs in the other direction brings you to Bridlington's harbour (and heritage museum), where large quantities of lobster and crab are now being landed, with many places to sample them.

A bit further afield, about 3 miles from Sewerby, is the RSPB Bempton Cliffs reserve. These towering chalk cliffs are home to many thousands of nesting seabirds, including gannets, kittiwakes and puffins (from April to August). It's just off National Route 1 on the way to Scarborough, and there's a train station in the village.

If you managed to catch a sunset over Morecambe Bay, then staying over to catch the sunrise over Bridlington Bay makes a perfect end to this trip; and a great time to start planning your next one!

PLACES TO STAY

There are a few places along this section and plenty of choice in Bridlington.

Nafferton
Star Inn 01377 255548
Nether Lane Bunk Barn 01377 241711 (budget option)
Harpham
St Quintin Arms 01262 490329
Bridlington
South Lodge Guest House 01262 671040
Swandale Guest House 01262 603966
Swallow Hotel 01262 679301
Expanse Hotel 01262 675347
Flamborough
Manor House 01262 850943

BIKE SHOPS & REPAIRS

Bridlington
Chain Cycles (01262 677555) just south of the route as it crosses St John's Street

B1229

Bempton

A165

Boynton

B1253

② Rudstone

③

Gypsey Race

Carnaby

④

Haisthorpe

A614

A165

BR

Kilham

Burton Agnes

① Thornholme

B1249

Ruston Parva

Thornholme

Harpham

DRIFFIELD

Lowthorpe

Fraisthorpe

A614

Nafferton

Kelk Beck

Great Kelk

Wansford

B1249

Skerne

Foston
on the
Wolds

A164

Skerne Beck

River Hull

Hutton
Cranswick

Watton

Image © Sustrans

Image © Cooper Douglas

60

ON

THINGS TO SEE

1 Burton Agnes Hall & Gardens

Elizabethan home lived in by the same family for more than four hundred years. Built 1598 -1610, and described by Simon Jenkins, author of England's Thousand Best Houses, as 'the perfect English house'. Tearoom (admission charge for Hall only) and toilets (closed Jan, Mar and early Nov).

2 Rudston Monolith

At over 7.6 metres (25ft) it's the largest free-standing Neolithic stone in Britain. Standing close to the Norman church, the stone is thought to have been erected around 1600 BC. Fossilised dinosaur footprints on one side possibly significant to those who erected it.

3 Bayle Museum and Priory Church

Next to the church, and once the entrance to Bridlington Priory, the only surviving parts from Henry VIII's destructive dissolution. Interesting interactive local history exhibits in the Old Town quarter. Small admission charge for adults (open Apr-Sept).

4 Harbour Heritage Museum

Models, photographs and other maritime memorabilia. 'Three Brothers' traditional sailing coble afloat outside. Small admission charge (open Apr-Oct).

5 Sewerby Hall ▼

Fine 18th century house on a cliff top location overlooking Bridlington Bay. One room dedicated to Hull born pioneering aviator Amy Johnson. Small zoo, aviary and various gardens. Admission charged, tearoom and toilets (open Easter –Sept).

Image © Gordon Ball LRPS/Shutterstock.com

Other coast-to-coast rides

If you've enjoyed *Way of the Roses*, there are five other coast-to-coast routes to try in the North of England. For more details about these and other long distance routes on the National Cycle Network, visit *www.sustrans.org.uk*

Reivers Cycle Route

172 miles (278km): Whitehaven – Tynemouth

Hadrian's Cycleway

174 miles (280km): Ravenglass – South Shields

Sea to Sea (C2C) Cycle Route

136 miles (219km): Whitehaven/Workington – Sunderland/Tynemouth

Walney to Wear & Whitby

152 miles (245km): Barrow in Furness – Sunderland
179 miles (288km): Barrow-in-Furness – Whitby

Way of the Roses

170 miles (274km): Morecambe – Bridlington

Trans Pennine Trail

215 miles (346km): Southport – Hornsea